Animal Totem:

Spiritual & Magical Powers of Mammals, Birds, Insects, and Fish

By: Kristina Benson

Animal Totem: Spiritual & Magical Powers of Mammals, Birds, Insects, and Fish

ISBN 13: 978-1-60332-017-7

Printed in the United States of America

Table of Contents

INTRODUCTION

Healers and spiritual leaders in tribal societies, also called
Shamans, have long believed that animals had special
properties, and could channel various spiritual energies.
The first shamanistic cultures developed in northern Asia,
but it is only in the 1700s, Shamanism was given a
universal usage in spoken language.

Every Shaman has at least one Guardian Spirit or Power
animal. He or she can meditate on this animal and absorb
the power of the entire species of that animal, even if one is
not physically present. When a Power Animal is in a
Shaman's possession, or is a companion of the Shaman, it
acts as an alter ego for the Shaman, giving the Shaman
transformative powers. Shamans use, and communicate
with, not only animals that are regarded as "real" by
Westerners, but also animals that have been relegated by
Westerners to mythical status. These animals can include
Dragon, Unicorn, and Gryphon, among others.

It is not necessary to be a Shaman, or to even aspire to be a
Shaman, to have, and benefit from, contact with animal
spirits. Shamans believe that everyone has power animals
which function kind of like a guardian angel. Each power
animal that you have increases your power so that illnesses

or negative energy cannot enter your body. The spirit also lends you the wisdom of its kind. This book will teach you how to identify your Power Animals, and how to channel the spirit of other members of the animal kingdom in order to amplify the benefits of meditation, and various spiritual practices. It may take time and patience, but eventually, everyone can find his or her animal spirit guides.

While Shamanism and Native American spirituality have experienced somewhat of a renaissance in the West, there are many other religions that honor animal spirits as well. The honoring of animal spirits is called Animism, and can be found the world over. Animism is perhaps one of humanity's oldest beliefs. Deriving from the Latin word Anima (meaning breath, or soul) this is the belief that everything in nature has its own soul, spirit or divinity. This can include non animals, such as rocks, mountains, or lakes. These animals and entities do not passively exist, but rather absorb and reflect the energy around them.

I. HOW DO I FIND MY POWER ANIMAL?

Power Animals are usually a reflection of our deepest selves, our spirits, and our souls. They also represent qualities which we may not even be aware that we have. Your personal Power Animal may change depending upon your specific needs. If you are dispirited, your animal is far away from you and needs to be called back, or replaced with another, willing Animal spirit.

All animals—even those thought of as vermin—have gifts to give, and are potentially positive spirits. Your Power Animal can talk to you, in words or in feelings, and will understand you. This animal is there to help you and, unlike a pet, doesn't need your care or guardianship.

In order to find your Power Animal, all you need is time, and patience.

Select a time where you can remain undisturbed. You will want to be somewhere quiet, and where you feel safe. If quiet is impossible to guarantee, you may use earplugs or noise canceling headphones, put on soothing, meditative music, or use a white noise machine.

Animal Totem

Once you have found a suitable time, make a pleasant space for yourself. Make sure that the room—or area (you can be outside if you want)—is free from distractions. Make sure that it is clean, and smells either neutral, or pleasant.

Now, you're ready to open yourself to your Power Animal. Lie down on your back, feet together at the ankles, tops of feet relaxing to fall outwards. Arms are at your sides, fingers relaxed. Breathe through your nose at a pace that is natural. Scan your body for tension or stiffness, and relax. Even the eyes, cradled in the sockets, should be still and relaxed.

Visualize yourself walking down a path. It can be night or day. The path can be through a meadow, in the snow, or in the desert. Whatever feels right to you is fine. The path leads to the opening of a cave. In the cave is your power animal. Sit outside the cave and wait as long as it takes for your animal to reveal itself.

When you see it, you will know. Do not send back your Animal if you are disappointed—say, if it's Cockroach, or Chicken. Sending him back will anger him, and is a product of the ego. Whichever animal you see is the one for you. When you see the Animal, take some time to get to know him or her. Is it a him or a her? What color? Is she old,

11

young? A parent? Will she let you touch her? Do you name the Animal, or does it already have a name?

When you are done getting to know your animal, or if he retreats back to the cave, remain in meditation for a while to reflect on what you just saw. When you are ready, open your eyes, breathe, and slowly sit up. Now you may look up your animal to see which properties he or she possesses, and how you can benefit.

It is certainly possible to have more than one Power Animal. In particularly trying times, it is also possible to actively call on animals for help. This will not offend your Power Animal, and he will still be yours even if another animal is coming to your aid.

During periods of difficulty or change, you may again want to go to your cave and see if your Power Animal is still there, or if a different animal emerges. Sometimes, your Power Animal will still be there. Others, a different Animal will have taken his place. This is your new Power Animal for the time being.

II. HOW CAN I CALL ON ANIMAL SPIRITS IF I NEED HELP?

Sometimes, your Power Animal's particular set of strengths will not help you meet a challenge. It is possible to retain your Power Animal while calling on another for help. There are four different types of Animal Guides that can come to your aid in times of trouble.

Messenger Guide: this animal quickly comes into your life and stays only long enough for you to figure out the message, and how it affects you. The message itself can be spiritual in nature, it can be a call to action, or it can be a warning. Sometimes the Animal will appear when you call to it for help; other times it will be sent to you, and it will be up to you to interpret why it was sent. For instance, you may see a nature program about a Lion. Then you might go for a walk and see a billboard advertising something with a Lion. Later that evening, a friend may mention something about drinks at the Red Lion Inn. It is possible that Lion is trying to send you a message, and will depart once you figure out what that message is.

A **Shadow Animal Guide** is one that scares you, such as a Cockroach, a Snake, or a large Dog. Its purpose it to teach a lesson that you may not have learned because of excessive hubris, or greed. A Shadow Guide will not stop returning until it inspires a change of action or lifestyle. For instance, you may be living an extraordinarily unhealthy lifestyle, and continue seeing or hearing about vultures at every turn. Until you make a change, you will continue seeing Vulture.

A **Journey Animal Guide** appears when you are forced to make a decision as to which path to take. It can be a friendly traveling companion if the path is right, and remains at your side until the journey is complete. It can be a friendly traveling companion if the path is right; if the animal is not friendly, call to your Power Animal for guidance to see if you've made the right decision.

Your **Power Animal** remains a part of you throughout large periods of time in your life, or even your entire life, and reflects your inner-spiritual self. You may have more than one and new ones may come during an expected time. Its powers are always there for you and serve as a constant reminder of your inner powers and oneness with nature.

III. HOW TO HONOR YOUR POWER ANIMAL

There are many ways to honor her. Honoring your Power Animal can be very personal, and it is possible that he will ask you what to do. Other times, it will be up to you to show your appreciation for your animal.

Wear Clothing or Jewelry Decorated With Images of Your Animal. You can also do this to constantly remind yourself of the powers that your animal gives you, and that he is always present for when you need him.

Research the Habits of Your Animal. Animals are fascinating creatures, with so much to teach us. Find out where your animal lives. Does he mate for life? What kinds of noises does he make, and what do they mean? Is her behavior as you expected?

Visit the Habitat of Your Animal. Visiting his home will help you connect with and understand him better than before.

Donate to Organizations that Protect Your Animal. Is his habitat threatened? Is he endangered? What can you do to make sure that this animal continues to be a part of Earth's community. Are there groups dedicated to him?

Animal Totem

For instance, a Parrot Enthusiast group, or a Friends of the Whale club near you? Find out how you can help your animal.

Visit Your Animal. This can be done when you meditate, or you can physically go see your animal. Sometimes you can go outside your own house and see him, depending on where you live. Other times, you may have to go to a zoo, or a wildlife preserve.

IV. ANIMALS

Each animal's strengths have been described, as well as situations where you may benefit from its guidance.

MAMMALS:

BAT

Many people are afraid of Bat, as in the West, they are closely associated with vampires. But in Tonga and West Africa and is often considered the physical manifestation of a soul, and are regarded as sacred. Among some Native Americans, such as the Creek, Cherokee and Apache, Bat is a trickster, and Bat mythology usually references his cunning and wit. In Chinese mythology, the bat is a symbol of longevity and happiness, and in Poland and parts of the Arabian Peninsula, is considered lucky.

Bat is nocturnal, and sleeps during the day. He is able to see at night using sonar, and has almost no use for his eyes. He is one of the few mammals that can fly, and can be a joy to watch when he emerges from the trees and caves at dusk.

Bat helps to move through cycles, some of which can involve loss, like death. Meditating on him can teach us to reorganize cultural biases, and find beauty in darkness.

BAT'S GIFTS

Ability to observe unseen, ability to connect with past lives, transition, death, rebirth.

BAT CAN HELP

When you need help in shedding the old and making peace with the new; to seek comfort when passing through darkness or shadows.

BEAR

There is evidence of prehistoric worship of bears, particularly in fishing and hunting tribes. In Korea, Finland, and Scandinavia there is mythology that suggest that the pre-historic peoples there regarded Bear as an ancestor, and in ancient Greece, the goddess Artemis was associated with the cult of the bear.

Most bears are active in the summer and spring, and hibernate in the winter. He has no natural predators, and though a fearful adversary, is gentle and tender with mates, and his young.

We can look to Bear to learn how to use our power and strength wisely, for patience, and for stillness.
BEAR'S GIFTS: Introspection, patience, comfort in solitude, wisdom, patience, astral travel.

BEAR CAN HELP WHEN: when you feel as though you are alone, in a shadow, and need patience in order to find your true path.

JAGUAR

The Jaguar is a new-world mammal, and one of four felines known as Big Cats. In Central and South America, the jaguar has long symbolized power and strength. The pre-Columbian Mesoamericans extensively used Jaguar motifs in artwork and sculpture, showing jaguars, humans with jaguar characteristics and humans wearing jaguar fur.

In the Maya civilization, the jaguar was believed to channel communication from the spirit world to the physical world. The Maya saw jaguars as their companions in the spiritual world, and kings were given a name incorporating the word jaguar.

The Aztecs also revered the jaguar for its strength and power, and formed an elite clan of warriors known as the Jaguar Knights. In Aztec mythology, the jaguar was considered to be the totem animal of the deity Tezcatlipoca.

A powerful and graceful feline, we can learn from his stealth and cunning. He has no natural predators, and at one time, could be found as far north as Southern California and Texas. Currently, powerful Jaguar is on the endangered species list.

JAGUAR'S GIFTS: Seeing roads through chaotic landscapes, understanding the patterns of chaos, bravery in darkness, empowerment, ability to traverse the unknown, shapeshifting, psychic sight.

JAGUAR CAN HELP: when you are having trouble seeing your path or purpose, or are fearful of a necessary spiritual journey.

ORCA

Art made by some indigenous peoples in the Pacific Northwest--such as the Kwakwaka'wakw, Coast Salish, Nuu-chah-nulth, and Tlingit—have created artwork that highlights the importance of Orca in their cultures.

In Siberian Yupik mythology, the wolf and the Orca were thought to be manifestations of the same animal: Orcas were said to appear as wolves in winter, and wolves as Orcas in summer. In the summer, Orca were believed to help assist the sea hunter in capturing walrus. To give thanks for this aid, small sacrifices were sometimes made to Orcas. Valuable plants, such as tobacco, were thrown in the sea as an offering to the Orca.

Although not central to Western mythology, Orcas, and Orca-like creatures, makes appearances in literature. One first appears in English in Michael Drayton's *Polyolbion*, an epic poem about Brutus the Trojan, the legendary founder of Great Britain. It also eventually appears in John Milton's epic poem *Paradise Lost*.

Also known as the Killer Whale, the Orca is the largest species of the dolphin family. It is found in all the world's oceans, from the Arctic and Antarctic regions to the Carribbean.

Though predators, the Orca poses no threat to humans. We can learn from Orca's gentle use of his strength, and his ability to adapt to all varieties of habitat.

ORCA'S GIFTS: Creation, freedom of the soul, finding soul's songs, seeing the unseen, soul memory, rainfall energy.

CALL ON ORCA: when you feel weighted down, or burdened; when you need help finding a solution to what seems like a simple problem.

COUGAR

The Native peoples of both North and South America have valued the cougar for his strength and stealth. The Inca city of Cusco is reported to have been designed in the shape of a Cougar, and the sky and thunder god of the Inca, Viracocha, has been depicted as a cougar.

In North America, descriptions of the Cougar have appeared in the mythologies of the Winnebago, Wisconsin and Cheyenne tribes. Cougar also has significance to the Apache and Walapai of Arizona, who say that the cry of the Cougar was a warning of impending death.
To this day, the Cougar, also known as a Puma, is representative of strength, stealth, and power.

COUGAR'S GIFTS: Southwest Indian tribes know Cougar as the Master Hunter, known for its high intelligence, his knowledge of other animal and life forms, his physical prowess, his strength of will, and his intuition.

CALL ON COUGAR: to help in better understanding adversaries, to help develop strategies for meeting particularly difficult challenges; balancing power, intention, strength, self-esteem, freedom from guilt, cunning.

WOLF

Traditionally, Western Europeans feared wolves, and middle European literature and folktales reflect this view. Settlers brought this view with them as they came to the New World, and the gray wolf, once ubiquitous in North America, was amongst the first species to dwindle in number after the arrival of the Europeans. As technology made the killing of wolves and predators easier, humans began to over hunt wolves and cause their numbers to dwindle significantly.

In Central Asian nations, the wolf is not feared, but revered. The pre-historical Turkic peoples even believed they were descendants of wolves. There is an old Turkic folklore that tells the story of a small village in China that was raided by Chinese soldiers. One small baby survived. A she-wolf named Asena, with a sky-blue pelt, found the baby and nursed him. They then eventually copulated, and from their union sprung the Turkish people. Greek mythology says that two babies, Romulus and Remus, were abandoned and then suckled by a she-wolf. Romulus then went on to found Rome.

Oddly, there are fewer reports of wolf attacks in North America than in Europe and Asia. In colonial India, in 1878, there were reports of 624 wolf attacks on humans. In Iran, there are several reports of wolves carrying small children away.

It is possible that wolves in Asia and Europe are of a different genetic stock that makes them more aggressive than wolves in the Americas, or it is possible that they were hunted more aggressively in the Old World and ergo, learned to fear humans.

WOLF GIFTS: outwitting enemies, ability to pass unseen, skill in protection of self and family, cunning, escape, ability to pass dangers, outwitting, wisdom, hunting and seeking, magick, dreams, introspection, intuition, listening, death and rebirth, transformation.

CALL ON WOLF: Guidance in dreams and meditations. Remember, Wolf is a very powerful animal spirit.

LYNX

In tribal communities, the Lynx has been described as a knower of secrets, with skills that include divination and clairvoyance.

A type of feral cat, the lynx is a cunning, solitary hunter, with large eyes and a keen sense of hearing. The lynx has also played a role in European mythology: it was chosen as the emblem of the Accademia dei Lincei ("Academy of the Lynxes"), and in medieval folktales, the Lynx was though to be able to turn its urine into a garnet.

Though not aggressive, the lynx is a loner, and secretive. If you call on him, he may appear, but you may face a challenge in getting him to cooperate.

LYNX'S GIFTS: Keenness of sight, divination, developing psychic senses, keeping secrets, moving through time and space.

LYNX CAN HELP: to help in understanding potential obstacles in your path, to aid in identifying potential adversaries.

COYOTE

The coyote often appears in Native American mythology, usually as a male, anthropomorphic character, that appears in often times highly sexually charged stories. He often plays the role of trickster, is usually clever, and occasionally funny. His fatal flaws often include greed, desire, recklessness, impulsiveness and jealousy. In Tongva Mythology, Coyote challenges "The River" to a race. He indeed wins, but collapses from fatigue. The river laughs at him, thus explaining why the noise made by the upper Arroyo Seco sounds similar to laughing.

Coyote is also a prominent character in some Native American creation mythologies. In one myth, Coyote kicks a ball of mud until it turns into the first man. In another myth Coyote is able to successfully impregnate an evil woman who has killed off all the other men in the world.

Coyote is a close relative of the Gray Wolf, and is occasionally portrayed in Indian mythology as Wolf's brother. The Coyote's natural habitat is extensive. They can be found in Mexico, Canada, and just about everywhere in between. They live in packs, and though diurnal in the wild, are nocturnal in urban and suburban settings, out of necessity.

COYOTE GIFTS: Balance between risk and safety, trust in truth, ability to laugh at one's own mistakes, letting go of walls that prevent us from accepting psychic energies, trickery, cunning, shape-shifting, stealth, opportunity, illumination, truth, creativity.

CALL ON COYOTE: help in learning to trust in oneself, guidance in determining how much of oneself to reveal to others, help in turning a crisis into an opportunity.

RABBIT

In Pagan cultures, Rabbit has been associated with fertility and spring, an example of which is the Easter Bunny. In Aztec mythology, a council of four hundred rabbit gods known represented fertility and parties. In Ojibwa mythology, the Great Rabbit, is an important deity related to the creation of the world.

The rabbit also appears in other tribes' Native American folklore as the trickster archetype, and in Chinese mythology as one of the 12 celestial animals in the Zodiac.

In Japanese tradition, rabbits live on the Moon where they make mochi, a delicious snack made from sticky rice, and occasionally ice cream. In the folklore of the United States, a rabbit's foot is thought to bring luck. The practice derives from the system of African-American folk magic similar to voodoo. In Jewish folklore, rabbits are associated not with fertility or parties, but with cowardice.

RABBIT'S GIFTS: Quickness, transformation, receiving hidden teachings and intuitive messages, quick thinking when necessary, letting go of a fear of disaster or illness, strengthening intuition.

CALL ON RABBIT: assistance in interpreting your way or path; help in letting go of fears and anxiety stemming from past events.

POLAR BEAR

The polar bear is the most carnivorous member of the bear family. Though often depicted in popular culture as a sort of an overgrown teddy bear, it is the bear species that is most likely to prey on humans. Polar Bears feed mainly on seals, but will also eat birds, rodents, shellfish, crabs, beluga whales, walruses, musk oxen, reindeer, and very occasionally other polar bears.

They are also swimmers and have been spotted 60 miles away from land. They are big, aggressive, curious, and as of late, have developed a taste for garbage. Due to global warming, the polar bear has recently been added to the endangered species list.

POLAR BEAR'S GIFTS: Ability to navigate along the Earth's magnetic lines, introspection, solitude, swimming through emotional waters, finding sustenance where there is none to be seen, strength in the face of adversity, defense and revenge

POLAR BEAR CAN HELP: when experiencing strife in personal relationships; when preparing to spend long periods of time alone; to determine the best course of action when wronged or mistreated.

MOLE

Moles live underground in an ornate labyrinth of tunnels and burrowing holes, and as such, are extremely agile, and comfortable in dark places. Some species can swim. Moles can be found in North America, Europe, Asia and the eastern seaboard of Australia.

Male moles are called boars; females are called sows. A group of moles is called a *labour*.

MOLE GIFTS: Familiarity with lower regions, ability to turn inward, blindness to all but light and dark in the material world, sensitivity to touch and vibration, understanding of earth energies.

MOLE CAN HELP: when it is necessary to do intensive research; when experiencing problems with intimacy with a partner.

DEER

Deer have been used in mythology since the Paleolithic era. Cave paintings from that era have been found depicting a shaman wearing deer antlers. The Insular Celts worshiped the Flidais, a deer goddess, and the Continental Celtics' artwork depicts deer antlers in paintings and upon altars. The horned god shown in these works is most likely one of the sources from which Wiccans conjured the figure of their Horned God. In Norse mythology, stags and deer figure prominently as characters in stories. In Slavic folk tales, the Golden-horned deer is a large deer with golden antlers. In Greek mythology, the deer is associated with Artemis in her role as virginal huntress, and draws her chariot.

Deer appear in Eastern traditional stories as well. In Jewish mythology exists a giant stag by the name who resides in a mythical forest called "Divei Ilai".

Deer are considered messengers to the Gods in Shinto, and in Hindu mythology, the goddess Saraswati takes the form of a red deer

In the New World, archetypes of the deer are found in the mythologies of the native peoples. For the Huichol people of Mexico, the "magical deer" represents both the earthly blessing of corn and the spiritual blessing of peyote. The Huichol hunt and sacrifice deer in their ceremonies and make offerings to the deer spirits.

Deer are widely distributed, and hunted, with indigenous colonies of deer existing in all continents except Antarctica and Australia. They can adapt to a range of habitats, and are herbivores.

DEER'S GIFTS: Gentleness in word, thought and touch, listening skills, grace and beauty, survival instinct, ability to sacrifice for a higher cause, connection to the wood spirits, swiftness, gentleness, avoiding force to achieve goals, alertness, scavenging, seeking, abundance, dreams, intuition, introspection, listening, death and rebirth, transformation.

DEER CAN HELP: when experiencing familial strife; when budget and resources are running low or stretched thin; when a child or youngster is in particular need of guidance or attention.

OTTER

Otter figure into some stories in Norse mythology. One character, the dwarf Ótr, takes the form of an Otter. The word Otter came from the Old Icelandic word *Otr*.

In some Native American cultures, otters are totem animals. They are carnivorous, and live in just about every corner of the world. A group of otters is called a "romp."

OTTER'S GIFTS: Connection with the inner child, faith, connection with goddess healing energies.

OTTER CAN HELP: when depressed or drained of energy.

FOX

In many cultures, the fox appears in folklore as a symbol of cunning and trickery, or as a familiar animal possessed of magic powers. This is true in Eastern mythology as well: Chinese folktales depict female foxes leading men away from their wives. The Chinese word for fox spirit is the same as the word for "mistress" in an extramarital affair.

In Japanese folklore, the fox Kitsune is a powerful animal spirit which is both mischeivious and cunning. Fox is a general term applied to species of small to medium-sized feral dogs with sharp features and a brush-like tail. By far the most common species of fox is the Red Fox.

FOX'S GIFTS: Shapeshifting, cleverness, ability to watch without being seen, connection with warrior goddess, stealth, swiftness, patience.

FOX CAN HELP YOU: to observe others around you without being perceived; when impatient about a plan; when needing the ability to act quickly and quietly.

DOLPHIN

Dolphins appear in a number of Greek myths, invariably as kind spirits that aid humans when in distress. There is a story about a dolphin rescuing the poet Arian, and at the temple to Poseidon, there is a statue of Arian riding on the back of his rescuer.

Another Greek myth has Dionysus turning pirates into dolphins so they do not drown.

In Hindu mythology the Ganges River Dolphin is associated with the goddess Ganga. The dolphin is said to be among the creatures which accompanied the goddess in her descent from the heaven.

The Boto people of the Amazon river envision dolphins as shapeshifters whom are capable of having children with human women.

DOLPHIN'S GIFTS: Connection with the water spirits, change, wisdom, balance, harmony, trust, connection with the rhythms of the ocean.

DOPHIN CAN HELP: in need of seeking a work/life balance; when psychic walls and barriers have been erected that block positive energies; to connect with the monthly cycle.

PORCUPINE

Porcupines are the fourth largest rodents in the world. All species and subspecies have modified hairs that serve as sharp spikes, or quills, to defend them against predators. They are found in Europe, Asia, and the Americas.   They are herbivores, and are diurnal.

PORCUPINE'S GIFTS: Defense, neutrality, wonder, trust, innocence.

PORCUPINE CAN HELP: you are trying to determine the appropriate ratio of trust and wariness to bring to a new relationship or situation.

RAM

In the Mediterranean area and Great Britain, sheep (or ram) are the most common type of livestock in pastoral farming.

The symbol of a sheep appears frequently in both Western and Eastern arts and culture. Judaism uses many sheep references, the best known of which may be the Passover lamb. Christianity uses sheep-related metaphors, such as referring to Christ as a Shepard, the Agnus Dei, and images of the lion lying down with the lamb. It is also worth noting that Abraham, Jacob, Moses, and King David all worked as shepherds. Sheep also are featured in Arab culture and mythology. Eid ul-Adha is a major annual festival in Islam in which a sheep is sacrificed.

The ram is also the first sign of the Western zodiac—Aries-- and forms one of the animals associated with the 12-year cycle of in the Chinese zodiac.

RAM'S GIFTS Maintaining balance, confidence, fertility, courage, abundance, assurance.

RAM CAN HELP: if having difficulty with fertility issues; for courage in the face of adversity; for assistance in balancing the desire to give to others with the need to take care of the self.

OPOSSUM

Also known as a "possum", this animal is a medium-sized marsupial that can get about as big as a large house cat. Their name comes from the Algonquin word "wapathemwa". They are able to adapt easily to a broad range of habitats because they can, and will, eat just about anything. When threatened, they immediately foam at the mouth, release a horrible smelling spray from their anal glands, and become stiff and curled. This catatonic state is an involuntary reaction. They will generally snap out of it if left alone, in a quiet place. Though not a particularly vicious opponent to any adversary, Opossum's strength is in his defense—he is immune to the bite of Rattlenake and Cottonmouth, and indeed most pit vipers.

OPOSSUM'S GIFTS: Deception, use of appearance, recovery, cunning.

OPOSSUM CAN HELP: to rediscover a lost path or way; to develop a better pokerface.

RACCOON

Raccoon has been part of Japanese mythology for thousands of years. "Takuki" is the Japanese name for Raccoon, which translates literally to "Raccoon-dog". The character, in mythology, is prone to mischief, disguise, and shapeshifting. Though kind, he is a bit gullible and scatter-brained. In Native American folklore and mythology. The Raccoon is the trickster and is the survivor, who lives alongside man as if to show him that he cannot truly conquer the land.

RACOON'S GIFTS: Disguise, dexterity, seeking guidance and confidence, curiosity, ability to question without fear.

RACOON CAN HELP: to get strength to stand up for what is right; for guidance in trying to uncover widespread deceit.

GOAT

Goats seem to have been first domesticated about 10,000 years ago in the Zagros Mountains of Iran. Domestic goats were generally kept in herds that wandered on hills or other grazing areas, tended by shepherds that would keep watch over the flock.

Historically, goat hide has been used for water bottles, wine bottles, and parchment.

Goats are mentioned many times in the Bible, and were considered clean animals, fit for slaughter in the honor of an important guest. It was also acceptable for some kinds of sacrifices. On Yom Kippur, the festival of the Day of Atonement, two goats were chosen and lots were drawn for them. One was sacrificed and the other allowed to escape, carrying with him the sins of the community. From this comes the word "scapegoat".

And, of course, in Greek mythology, the trickster Pan was alleged to be half goat, and half human.

GOAT: Abundance, independence, surefootedness, agility, stubbornness.

CALL ON GOAT: tempted to waver from what you know to be right in favor of what you know to be easy.

SKUNK

The striped skunk's scientific name "mephitis mephitis" means "noxious gas, noxious gas". A skunk's first line of defense is the two musk glands located on either side of the anus which let go a smelly yellow spray that can hit targets as far as 12 feet away. Before spraying, the skunk will stamp its feet, erect its tail, hiss, and then spray. The skunk is technically a rodent and eats bird eggs, fruit, and small insects. Although the most common fur color is black and white, some skunks are brown or gray, and a few are cream-colored. All skunks are striped, even from birth.

SKUNK'S GIFTS: Reputation, creativity, courage, will-power, confidence.

SKUNK CAN HELP: when desiring creative solution to a challenge; for strength in sticking to a rigorous physical, emotional, or spiritual workout regimen.

ARMADILLO

Animals have various methods of protecting themselves. These methods come instinctively, and are often used in life-or-death situations. Humans have similar instincts but have to navigate a complex culture in which it is not always appropriate to fight, or flee.

Many of us fear that if we set boundaries, we'll sabotage our careers, friendships, and families. During childhood, attempts to protect oneself can be met with scorn from adults. Many of us, especially women, never really learn to set and stick by a boundary.

Armadillo means "little armored one" in Spanish, and its armor consists of overlapping bony plates, covered by horns. When scared, Armadillo rolls up in a little ball for protection. Not quite fleeing, but definitely not fighting. Meditating on Armadillo medicine can help to guide us in terms of appropriate boundaries. He can also teach us that armor can protect us from the outside, but not the inside.

ARMADILLO'S GIFTS: Ability to protect oneself, understanding vulnerabilities, respect for boundaries, empathy, determination

ARMADILLO CAN HELP: when feeling spiritually or psychically vulnerable; when facing difficulty relating to others who have different points of view.

WEASEL

In Japanese mythology there exists malevolent, weasel-like wind spirits, wielding sickles and working in groups of three to harm victims. Weasels, in traditional Japanese storytelling, represent sickness, bad luck, and death.

WEASEL: Stealth, cunning, ingenuity, revenge, trickery.

CALL ON WEASEL: to get assistance when motivated to take a vengeful path.

BEAVER

Beavers are native to North America, and are a semi-aquatic species of rodent. They work in groups to dam rivers and create estuarine environments in which to live. According to Chelan Native American creation mythology, the Maker created the animals and named them. He promised to return, and when he did, he found that some animals were complaining about their names. He decided not to make a Human, as he had originally promised, and instead, made Beaver, telling the animals that if they followed instructions, he would one day turn into a Human. He left Coyote in charge. Eventually, after a series of mishaps, Beaver was infused with the breath of life, and became Human.

BEAVER'S GIFTS: Productivity, resourcefulness, creativity, power over one's environment, dexterity, understanding the power of the group.

BEAVER CAN HELP: when working in a group setting; when called upon to adapt to a particularly difficult environment.

MOOSE

Moose is the largest member of the deer family, and can be found in the Northern parts of the Northern Hemisphere. According to the Inuit peoples, Moose almost destroyed the river when he drank too much water. In Lapp astrology, there is a constellation that depicts a moose hunt.

European rock drawings and cave paintings tell us that the elk or moose has been hunted since the stone age. In Scandinavia one can still find remains of trapping pits used for hunting elk. These pits would have been hidden with branches and leaves. The moose would fall through the pit, and be unable to get out due to the steep, slippery sides. The pits are normally found in large groups, crossing the elk's regular paths and stretching over several kilometers. Trapping elk in pits is an extremely effective hunting method, and as early as the 16th century the Norwegian government tried to restrict their use. Nevertheless, the method was in use until the 19th century.

MOOSE'S GIFTS: Strength, wisdom, respect for elders, stillness.

MOOSE CAN HELP: to find peace in stillness and tradition

SEAL

There are several types of seals, including Grey Seals, Hooded Seals, Monk Seals, Elephant Seals, and Crabeater Seals. They are ocean-dwelling mammals primarily found in the Northern Hemisphere. Some make a distinct barking noise to communicate; others slap the water and grunt. They primarily live on fish, in saltwater environments, and are protected from the cold by thick fur, and a layer of blubber.

SEAL'S GIFTS: Constancy of spirit during change, connection with the dream world, protection from danger, creativity.

SEAL CAN HELP: to surrender to necessary change, to find meaning in dreams, to fortify yourself against a particularly taxing spiritual challenge.

HEDGEHOG

Currently, the only living native hedgehogs are in Europe
and Asia. No native species are currently in North or South
America. Hedgehogs are easily distinguished by their
spines, which are stiff, hollow hairs. They come out when a
hedgehog sheds baby spines and replaces them with adult
spines. When under extreme stress or during sickness, a
hedgehog will lose spines. They are not as sharp as
porcupine quills, and not as easily removed from the
animal. Hedgehogs were eaten in Ancient Egypt and some
recipes of the Late Middle Ages call for hedgehog meat.
They primarily eat insects, and the eggs of birds.

In eastern Africa, the skin or spines of the White Bellied
hedgehog is regarded as a fertility charm. If a hedgehog's
skin is placed on seed in advance of planting, it will bring
good luck to the harvest. At one time, it was believed that
eating hedgehogs would cure the sick of all sorts of
ailments including leprosy, colic, boils, stones and poor
vision.

The gypsies of Europe still eat hedgehogs as a cure for
poisoning and, perhaps even, for removing evil spells..

HEDGHOG GIFTS: Wisdom of female elders, fertility, connection with the weather.

HEDGEHOG CAN HELP: When in need of guidance to a particularly complex problem; before filling the role of a mentor or mother.

COW/BULL

Cows, or cattle, are raised as livestock for meat, dairy products, and also used as work animals. In some countries, such as India, they are honored in religious ceremonies and revered. Currently, there is one cow for every six people on this earth. Cattle figure prominently in aspects of Christian mythology. St Luke is often depicted as an ox, and in Numbers, it is stated that the ashes of a sacrificed, unblemished heifer can be used for purification purposes.

The cow makes an appearance in both the Chinese Zodiac, and as the constellation Taurus. Cows are also given a special, revered status within the Hindu religion of India. According to Vedic scripture they are to be treated with the same respect 'as one's mother' because of the milk they provide. They appear in numerous stories from the Puranas and Vedas, for example the deity Krishna is brought up in a family of cow herders, and given the name Protector of the Cows. In ancient rural India every household had a few cows which would provide milk, and be used as work animals.

COW'S GIFTS: Love, sharing through community, connection to earth spirits, contentment, peace, tranquility, stillness.

COW CAN HELP: to get through family gatherings; to aid in desires to simplify or unclutter; if agitated or in need of relaxing; when kids or pets are posing a challenge.

MOUSE

The mouse is a small rodent that currently lives in nearly every country on Earth. Because of its ability to adapt to almost any climate, the mouse is regarded to be the third most successful mammalian species living on Earth today, after humans and the rat. The mouse is the oldest recognized species of mammal, and was written about in ancient Rome. In 1100 BC, descriptions of white mice appear in Chinese texts, but it is possible that white mice were discovered long before that in ancient Rome. Mice appear in Welsh and Lapp mythology as mischief makers.

MOUSE: Shyness, quietness, attention to detail, invisibility, discovery, ability to be unseen.

CALL ON MOUSE: to get help being a better listener; when there is a need to be particularly watchful while remaining calm; when there is a benefit to blending into the crowd.

PIG

Pigs are in the swine family and are native to Eurasia. They have been making appearances in mythology and folklore for thousands of years. In ancient Egypt pigs were associated with Set, the rival to the sun god Horus.

The Celts had a god of swine called Moccus, who under Roman occupation was merged somewhat with Mercury. In Celtic mythology, a cauldron overflowing with cooked pork was one of the attributes of The Dagda, and in Greek mythology, Demeter was the goddesss of pigs.

The Abrahamic religions diverge in opinion when it comes to pigs. The dietary laws of Judaism and Islam consider pigs unclean, and inappropriate to consume as food. Seventh-day Adventists and some other fundamental Christian denominations also consider pork forbidden, but Catholics and other more mainstream Christian sects consider pigs appropriate to eat. In fact, in Catholicism, Eastern Orthodoxy and other older Christian groups, pigs are associated with Saint Anthony, the patron saint of swineherds. As such, during both the Spanish Inquisition and Portuguese Inquisition, pork became a mainstay of many dishes and those who would not eat it—Jews and Muslims—were called "marranos."

In Hinduism the god Vishnu took the form of a boar in order to save the earth from an evil spirit who had dragged it to the bottom of the ocean, and in ancient Greece, a sow was an appropriate sacrifice to Demeter and had been her favorite animal.

The pig is one of the 12-year cycle of animals which appear in the Chinese zodiac related to the Chinese calendar. Believers in Chinese astrology associate each animal with certain personality traits. The sign of the Pig is one of the Earthly Branches, or zodiac signs, in Chinese astrology.

PIG'S GIFTS: Connection with deep earth, intelligence, cunning, ability to root out the truth.

PIG CAN HELP: if you feel that you are not being treated honestly; if it is necessary to talk someone in to giving a difficult truth.

DONKEY/BURRO

The donkey is a domesticated member of the horse family, and have been making appearances in folklore and myth for thousands of years. Several donkeys have been found buried in ancient Egyptian tombs, and the ass (a type of donkey) was a symbol of the Greek god Dionysus.

The Abrahamic texts also devote some words to the donkey. In the Hebrew bible, it is said that owning many donkeys is a sign of the lord's blessing. The bible often specifies if a person rode a donkey since it was an indicator of wealth. Horses, at that time, were used for war, and were even more expensive. In Numbers 22:22-41 "The Lord opened the mouth of the donkey" (vs. 28) and it speaks to Balaam. In Judges 15:13-17 where the hero Samson slays Philistines with the jawbone of an ass. Additional references can be found in Deuteronomy 22:10, Job 11:12, Proverbs 26:3 and elsewhere. In fact, the greek word for donkey appears about 100 times in the bible. Mary is often depicted riding on a donkey while pregnant with Jesus, and the messiah himself is often described as riding a donkey.

Donkeys appear to be quite intelligent, cautious, friendly, playful, and eager to learn. They are many times fielded with horses due to a perceived calming effect on nervous horses.

DONKEY'S GIFTS: Stubbornness, steadfastness, refusal to give up on ideals, courage, ability to put oneself first, disregarding the opinions of naysayers.

DONKEY CAN HELP: to strengthen resolve; to get the strength needed to take the right path over the easy one.

WOLVERINE

The wolverine is the largest land dweller of the weasel family, and is native to the northernmost parts of North America, Greenland, and Eurasia. The wolverine, though small, is strong, and omnivorous. The Innu people have a myth about the wolverine that explains the present location and size of a man's genitals. The Ojibway people also have a sexualized myth about Wolverine. In a story about two foolish young women who want to make love to the stars, they quickly become bored with their star husbands and call to wolverine to help them escape. He does, but first has sex with them before letting them go.

WOLVERINE'S GIFTS: Revenge, craftiness, gluttony, strength, ability to travel to the spirit world, strength to stand ground, trickery, cunning, endurance.

WOLVERINE CAN HELP: when it may become necessary to engage with an adversary; when refusing to compromise important values; to get sustenance through a potentially long period of conflict.

WALRUS

The walrus is a large, semi-aquatic mammal that lives in the coldest parts of the northern hemisphere. They primarily exist on ice floes, and live on small marine animals such as fish or clams. The male of the species has the largest penises of the animal kingdom, but it's completely internal. Despite their enormous size and short legs, they can run as fast as an adult human. They typically live in groups, and can stay underwater for as long as a half hour in waters 300 ft deep. Walruses have only two natural enemies: the orca and the polar bear. Polar bears hunt walruses by scaring them, and picking off the slowest members of the group.

Walruses use their long tusks (elongated canines) for fighting, dominance, display, and to dig holes in or anchor themselves to ice.

WALRUS' GIFTS: Understanding the power of appearing aggressive, preparing for the future, value in territory and community.

WALRUS CAN HELP: when it may be necessary to vigorously defend space, family, or property; when facing challenges in dealing with colleagues or family members.

RAT

The rat is a medium sized member of the rodent family that can be found in nearly every country on earth. They appear in poetry and mythology of the ancient Romans, though they were merely referred to as big mice.

In Imperial Chinese culture, the rat is the first of the twelve animals of the Chinese zodiac. People born in this year are expected to be creative, honest, generous, ambitious, and quick-tempered. In India, the Karni Mata Temple, the rats are held to be destined for reincarnation as Hindu holy men. The attending priests feed milk and grain to the rats, and they are permitted to run free. Eating food that has been touched by the animals is considered a blessing from god.

Western associations with the rat are generally negative, possibly from the association of rats with the 14th-century medieval plague called the Black Death. However many people in Western cultures keep rats as pets and find them to be tame, clean, intelligent, and playful.

RAT'S GIFTS: Abundant fertility, ability to live unseen, defense, cunning, shapeshifting.

CALL ON RAT: when attempting to start a large family or community; when forced to engage with a bigger and stronger adversary.

DOG

The dog is a domesticated subspecies of wolf, domesticated anywhere from 15,000 to 20,000 years ago. New evidence suggests that the Chinese were the first people to domesticate dogs, and the Chow chow, Shar Pei, Akita, Shiba Inu, and Basenji are amongst the dogs that they bred. In some parts of the world, the dog is regarded as a smaller, furrier member of the family. In others, the dog is merely a work animal. And in still others, dogs are considered unclean and not to be touched. Islamic law, for instance, considers dogs to be unclean because Muhammad is said to have given an order to kill all dogs in Medina. This particular hadith also states that the angel Gabriel does not enter a house where there are dogs.

In the Chinese Zodiac, the dog is the 11th animal. People born in the year of the dog are loyal, consistent, sympathetic, sensitive, loyal, impatient, and idealistic.

Those that interact with humans frequently regard people merely as other members of their pack. They are intelligent, loyal, and inquisitive. Today, according to the American Kennel club, the most popular dogs are Labradors, Terriers, and German Shepherds.

DOG'S GIFTS: Ability to heal emotional wounds in humans, ability to inspire trust, love, loyalty, love, protection.

DOG CAN HELP: when distraught; when facing challenges trusting people that clearly are friends or well-wishers; when wanting to inspire others to trust in you.

CAT

Cats have been domesticated since at least ancient Egypt, where the mythical cat Bast, the daughter of the sun god Ra, was goddess of the home. The domestic cat was most often used in order to protect of the fields, grain storehouses, and home from vermin infestations. Several other ancient religions believed that cats are souls, angels, companions, or guides for humans, and are omniscient. While in Islam there is not a sacred species, it is said by some writers that Muhammad had a favorite cat, Muezza, and that "[the Prophet] would do without his cloak rather than disturb one that was sleeping on it".

Living with humans is a symbiotic social adaptation which has developed over thousands of years. It is certain that the cat thinks of the human differently than it does other cats. Some have suggested that, psychologically, the human keeper of a cat is a sort of surrogate for the cat's mother.

Cat: Independence, connection with the female spirit, self love, ability to walk quietly, longevity.

Call on Cat: when rumors are swirling around you and you need the strength to shrug them off; when suffering from low self-esteem; when it is necessary to approach an adversary or opponent quietly or surreptitiously.

WILDEBEAST

The wildebeast is also called the gnu, and is a member of the antelope family. As such, the wildebeast is native to Africa. The name wildebeest finds its origin in the Dutch and Afrikaans words *wild* and *beest*, which mean "wild animal" and "beest" in Afrikaans means "cattle". The WIldebeast is a fairly docile animal that lives on the plains, feeding on grasses.

Wildebeast: Strength in numbers, understanding of the seasons, understanding the power of the group, grace.

Call on Wildebeast: to help form a community or supportive circle; to let go of pride and ask for help when necessary.

WOODCHUCK

Also known as a groundhog, the woodchuck is a rodent native to North America. They are active in the summer and spring, and hibernate during the cold fall and winter months. They are excellent at burrowing, using tunnels and burrows to sleep, rear young, and hibernate. The name for the animal stems from the Algonquin word for the animal—"wuchak."

Woodchuck: Connection with spirits of weather and climate, connection to rhythms and cycles of the earth, protection from floods and rain.

Call on Woodchuck: to meditate on the changing of the seasons; to cope with a sudden, dramatic change in weather.

PRARIE DOG

The prairie dog is a small rodent native to the North American grasslands and plains. They live in groups, and "bark" when danger approaches. The groups in which they live can be enormous, spanning hundreds of acres. Each family consists usually of a male and two to four females. They are sociable, friendly, and gentle, and currently are classified as a "keystone" species.

Prairie Dog: Value of play, connection to earth spirit, value of family and community.

Call on Prairie Dog: when endeavoring to start a new community or circle; to better appreciate the joy found in ordinary things.

MUSKRAT

The Muskrat is a large aquatic rodent native to North America. They primarily live in freshwater environments such as marshes, lakes, and ponds, and are very good swimmers. They live in packs, and occasionally inhabit beaver dams.

MUSKRAT'S STRENGHTS: Connection with the earth, adaptability, connection with others, ability to make treasure out of trash.

MUSKRAT CAN HELP: when dealing with a shortage of resources or change in financial circumstance; when faced with an abrupt and unplanned change of course.

CHIPMUNK

The word for this squirrel-like rodent may have come from the Odawa word jidmoonh, which translates literally to "red squirrel." These cute little creatures are omnivores, eating fruit, nuts, birds eggs, worms, and fungi. They are meticulously clean, and spend much of their time underground, in elaborate burrows. There are about 23 different species of animal that are considered "chipmunk", and are found throughout North America and parts of Europe.

CHIPMUNK'S GIFTS: Childhood, value in play, mobility, agility, ability to foresee the future, harmony with trees and plants.

CHIPMUNK CAN HELP WHEN: when feeling old and creaky; when preparing to interact with younger people; when constrained by living in the past instead of looking towards the future; whenever tempted to utter the words "in my day".

GUINEA PIG

The guinea pig is native to the Andes mountain range of South America, where it plays an important role in tribal diet and medicine. It was introduced to the West as a pet by European traders and explorers in the 1500s. Before becoming pets for Europeans and Americans, however, they were domesticated as long as 7000 years ago by tribes in present day central America. Today, households in that region still use them for food, and folk doctors use them to diagnose diseases such as jaundice, rheumatism, and arthritis by rubbing them against the bodies of the affected, and then being dissected. They are intelligent, gentle, playful animals, and make excellent companions and pets.

GUINEA PIG'S STREGNTHS: Simplicity, responsibility, strength of community, gentleness.

GUINEA PIG CAN HELP: if a simple problem doesn't seem to have an immediate solution; when preparing to ask others for help.

HORSE/PONY

Horses are social animals, and live in groups. They are generally gentle and inquisitive, first domesticated in Central Asia around 6,500 years ago. The horse is a member of the Chinese Zodiac, and it is said that those born in the year of the horse are independent, confident, quick-witted, inquisitive, and determined. They also are gifted, cunning, and like to be the center of attention. Horses also appear in Hindu mythology, where, according to legend, a white, winged horse emerged from the sea during the churning of the oceans. One of the gods took him to the celestial heavens, severed the wings, and sent the horse back to earth for humans to enjoy.

HORSE GIFTS: Power, stamina, endurance, freedom, travel, astral travel, cooperation, friendship.

HORSE CAN HELP: to gain stamina for a long physical or spiritual journey; to send positive energy to a faraway loved one.

SQUIRREL

The squirrel is a small, omnivorous rodent that is typically diurnal. The squirrel is a clever, stubborn animal, but with patience, they can acquiesce to being handled or hand fed.

Squirrel: Resourcefulness, agility, speed, ability to sense danger, planning, ability to prepare for future.

Call on Squirrel: for guidance in how to allocate surplus wealth or resources for the future; to absorb the energy necessary for functioning in a state of heightened urgency.

BADGER

There are eight species of badger, and belong to the same mammal family as ferrets and weasels. Their behaviors vary greatly: some are solitary, but some live in groups. They are omnivorous, and occasionally aggressive, though they are obviously too small to be any real threat to humans.

Badger: Keeper of stories, boldness, aggressiveness, cunning, passion, connection with earth spirits, creativity.

Call on Badger: when faced with adversity in the workplace; when planning to grow or nurture something; when there seems to be no solution to a challenge.

GIRAFFE

The giraffe is an African mammal. It is the tallest of all land-living animals. The giraffe has one of the shortest sleep requirements of any mammal averaging under 2 hours a day. Lions are the only predators which pose a serious threat to an adult giraffe.

GIRAFFE GIFTS: Clairvoyancey, Good sense of the future, strong ties to family and friends

CALL ON GIRAFFE: When you need balance and what to progress, when you need sight of the future.

BIRDS:

The modern bird first appeared in the late Jurassic period, and there are currently almost 10,000 living species of bird. Some, like the hummingbird, are tiny and can fly; others, like the ostrich, are large and flightless. All, however, have only two legs, lay eggs, have feathers, and are warm-blooded. Currently, 1200 or so species of bird are listed as endangered.

CROW

Crows are flock animals, though the correct term for a group of crows is not a flock but a "murder", and "crow" is usually also used to describe raven species. They are found in Australia, Africa, Europe, North America, South America, and Eurasia, and are remarkably intelligent. Some subspecies have been observed using tools on a regular basis, and others have been found using bread crumbs to bait-fish. Their natural predators are larger birds called "raptors".

Crows and ravens are often used in European literature and folklore as an omen for death, possibly because of their black plumage and penchant for eating carrion. The Raven also makes an appearance in Native American creation mythology, and in Norse mythology, Odin keeps two ravens as pets. In Irish mythology, crows are associated with battle, and English folklore says that England will fall if crows ever leave the tower of London.

CROW'S GIFTS: Ability to move in space and time, power of the ancestors, movement from darkness to light, bravery in shadows, bravery in darkness, bravery in the void, shapeshifting.

CROW CAN HELP: when you feel overwhelmed by darkness.

OWL

Owls are a solitary, nocturnal bird of prey. Ancient Egyptians used a picture of an owl to represent the sound "m". The Hopi Indians regarded owls as bad luck, and the Aztecs thought the owl to be a symbol of death and destruction.

In Eastern culture, the owl gets better press: in India, the white owl is an omen of prosperity and good luck, and in Japanese mythology, certain types of owls are divine messengers of the gods.
Because of their feather construction, owls are able to fly almost silently, and use this element of surprise to their advantage when hunting.

OWL GIFTS: Stealth, moon magick, silence, swiftness, secrecy, stealth, link between dark and light, understanding of shadow self, comfort in darkness.

OWL CAN HELP: when having difficulty coping with darkness or shadows; to connect with the feminine spirit; for aid in keeping secrets.

HERON

The heron is a long-legged bird that is also referred to as an Egret. This beautiful, graceful bird was perhaps the blueprint for the fictional Bennu bird in Egyptian mythology. The Bennu, which, in depictions looks remarkably like a Heron, was the sacred bird of Heliopolis, and associated with creation.

They mostly live in the wetlands, and eat frogs, fish, and other aquatic animals.

Heron: Dignity, self-reliance, pride, ability to set boundaries, stillness.
Call on Heron: to learn to be more independent and self confident; to learn how to put oneself first.

HUMMINGBIRD

Hummingbirds are delightfully tiny, hyper little creatures native only to the Americas. Some species can flap their wings 80 times per second. The smallest bird in the world is the Bee Hummingbird, which weighs only slightly over .06 ounces. They feast on nectar and have long, thin beaks and bifurcated tongues.

The Aztec God Huitzlopochtli is often rendered in drawings as a hummingbird, and Native Americans in Northern California credit Hummingbird with making fire.

HUMMINGBIRD'S GIFTS: Endurance over long journeys, happiness, love, relaxation, letting go of judgment, spontaneity.

HUMMINGBIRD CAN HELP: fortification of the spirit before embarking on a long physical or emotional journey; help in getting along with peers or coworkers; assistance in breaking out of a dull routine.

DUCK

Ducks are aquatic birds that can be found in both sea and freshwater. Some types of ducks can dive and hunt for food underwater. The downside to this ability to dive is that they have a hard time flying, and as such, are vulnerable to many types of predators.

Yokut mythology credits the duck with parting the sea from the sky, and Hungarian mythology has the sun taking the form of a golden diving duck to bring life to creatures at the bottom of the sea.

DUCK'S GIFTS: grace on water, water energy, connection with the water spirits.

DUCK CAN HELP: when on the cusp of embarking on a journey over water; to connect with water spirits after a heavy rainfall.

EAGLE

Eagles are primarily found in North America, though there are a few species in Australia. In Jewish tradition the eagle is a symbol of greatness, and te Torah compares God to an eagle in Deuteronomy.

The eagle also appears in the bible, used as a symbol for John the Apostle. In artistic renderings, John is often depicted with an eagle, which symbolizes the height he rose in the first chapter of his gospel.

Some Native American peoples revere eagles as sacred religious icons, and use Eagle feathers to honor noteworthy exceptional leadership and bravery. In the cultures of the Northwest Coast, Eagle is also a supernatural being. As such, United States eagle feather law stipulates that only individuals of certifiable Native American ancestry enrolled in a federally recognized tribe are authorized to obtain eagle feathers for religious or spiritual use.

EAGLE'S GIFTS: Swiftness, courage, strength, dignity, grace, ability to see the big picture, respect for boundaries, connection with spiritual over the material, perseverance.

EAGLE CAN HELP WHEN: too bogged down in small details to be able to see the larger arc of your path; when tempted to give up on a project or goal; to seek guidance in determining appropriate dynamics between you and your children or employees.

HAWK

The word "hawk" is used loosely to describe many different types of birds of prey. Those who fall under this classification are intelligent, fierce, and quick. They are believed to have vision that is about eight times as good as a human with very good eyesight. In ancient Egypt, hawks were regarded as royal birds, and many different gods were depicted with hawk heads. In Greek mythology, hawks were considered messengers of the sun god Apollo. Aztecs too considered hawks to be messengers from the gods, and the Lakota admired the hawk's speed and agility, and the Shawnee have legends about the hawk's place in the zodiac. The Hopi Indians have a myth in which Hawk rescues a kidnapped boy, The hawk also has been mentioned in Christian mythology, such as in Job, when God put Job in his place by asking him, "Does the hawk fly by your wisdom, and spread its wings toward the south?"

HAWK'S GIFTS: Connection with past lives, ability to traverse to spirit world, illumination, guardianship, truth, experience, clear-sightedness.

HAWK CAN HELP: when in need of spiritual guidance during a difficult time.

PELICAN

Pelicans are freshwater birds with arching necks and webbed feet. Some species of pelican fish in groups by herding fish into shallow water; others dive below the water's surface. In Medieval Europe, the Pelican was often a symbol of the Eucharist, and of the Passion of Christ. This in part rose from the pre-Christian legend that a pelican mother would let her babies drink her own blood rather than let them starve.

PELICAN'S GIFTS: Appropriate use of resources, control of ego, clear-headedness.

PELICAN CAN HELP: when struggling to deal with a promotion; when losing patience with children or employees.

VULTURE

Vultures are scavenger birds and feed primarily on carrion and animal carcasses. They exist on every continent except Antarctica and Oceania. Ancient Egyptians regarded vultures as excellent mothers and the vulture hieroglyph was used in words such as Mother and Grandmother. The Oleblbis people have a myth wherein two vultures were charged with making a ladder to the heavens. The Tembe people of Brazil have a tale involving a man who steals fire from the vultures and sets it in a tree. Cherokee mythology says that a buzzard created the mountains out of the sky, and the Seneca peoples have a myth wherein Vulture is stripped of his pretty plumage due to his vanity.

VULTURE'S GIFTS: Death, rebirth, prophecy, purification, connection with mother goddess.

CALL ON VULTURE: when dealing with the loss of a loved one; to seek guidance at the loss of a parent or guardian.

PENGUIN

Penguins are large, flightless birds that live primarily in the southern hemisphere. Possibly because their only predator, the seal, is at sea, they have little or no fear of humans that have approached them on foot. They are fairly awkward on land, but in water, using their wings as flippers, they are quite graceful and agile. Their eyes too have adapted to use underwater and they don't have very good vision when on land.

Some species of penguin mate for life; others, just for a season. Usually, the male is charged with guarding and incubating the egg while the female fetches food for him. They are flock animals, and live in large groups called "crèches."

PENGUIN'S GIFTS: Fatherhood, male nurturing, astral projection, endurance.

PENGUIN CAN HELP: for men: to get in touch with the ability to nurture and gently guide a youngster, child, or subordinate; for all—to send powerful psychic energy to far away loved ones; to prepare for a long or difficult physical journey.

WOODPECKER

According to Pawnee mythology, the woodpecker and the turkey once had a discussion as to which bird should be called the protector of humankind. The turkey argued that it should definitely be hers because she laid the largest clutch of eggs. However, the woodpecker argued that although she laid fewer eggs, the survival rate of her young was greater than that of the turkey's.In Greek mythology, Circe turned Picus, the Roman god of agriculture and manure, into a woodpecker because she was angry that he had her. Celeus was changed into a green woodpecker for attempting to steal honey from the baby Zeus. In Ancient Egypt, this bird was called the "Axe of Ishtar." Ishtar was the Babylonian goddess of fertility, love, and war. According to a Lakota legend, the red-headed woodpecker taught a poor young suitor how to make and play the first flute, and in European folklore, God called upon the birds to help Him dig rivers, lakes, and seas into the face of the earth, the woodpecker refused to join in. Because of this, it was forbidden to drink anything but rain and sentenced to peck wood.

WOODPECKER'S GIFTS: Connection to earth, ability to penetrate through barriers, connection to rhythm and patterns.

WOODPECKER CAN HELP: When called upon to dig through convoluted stories to find the truth; when trying to ascertain where you are in the cycle of the phase of life that you're in.

TURKEY

The turkey is a member of the pheasant family, and is native to the New World. The Aztecs domesticated the southern Mexican sub-species, which went on to spawn the domesticated turkey which is a popular main dish for the Thanksgiving holiday. The Pilgrims brought farmed turkeys with them from England, descendants of the original Mexican domesticated turkeys introduced into Europe by the Spanish, as they did not know that they were present as wild Turkeys in North America. To the Aztecs, the bird was sacred, and a festival would take place in honor of the bird every two hundred days. Turkeys were also domesticated by the Mayans, and were served to royalty as well as used in ceremonies for healing and planting. Turkeys are polygamous, and the male of the species is quite a bit bigger than the female.

TURKEY'S GIFTS: Sacrifice, giving, honors the Earth Mother.

TURKEY CAN HELP: to give you strength on the eve of a great sacrifice.

GULL

This carnivorous sea bird is intelligent, social, and resourceful. Some subspecies of gull survive by stealing food from other birds; others scavenge and hunt for themselves. The Innut people have a tale in which the seagull collaborates with Grandma Porcupine to save abducted bear cubs from a sea monster. The Cheyenne have a story wherein Seagull kept sunlight all to himself, until Raven tricked him out of it, and daylight met the world.

GULL'S GIFTS: Friendship, communication with the sky spirit, swiftness, harmony with the wind spirits.

Call on Gull: to achieve harmony with the weather; to help in bonding with a friend in need who is perhaps resistant to your advice and support.

BLUE JAY

The blue jay is a lavender-blue colored bird that lives primarily in the Eastern part of Canada and the United States. The Blue Jay is spectacularly bold and daring, even chasing away hawks and other large, predatory birds, and raids the nests of other birds to eat the eggs or chicks. There are many different stories about Blue Jay from a variety of Native American groups. In one, he is punished for the pride he took in his beautiful plumage. In another, he tricked a man into thinking he was the Great Spirit.

Blue Jay: Warning, courage, ability to spot potential challenges ahead.

Call on Blue Jay: when about to embark on a particularly difficult spiritual or physical journey; to get spiritual sustenance in times of trouble; to get inspired to seek solutions to arduous problems or challenges.

FINCH

These hyper, tiny birds are primarily found in Africa but species flourish in North America and Europe as well. The Goldfinch in particular is known for its bright yellow plumage, giving him the name Wild Canary. They are social, active little birds, and the domesticated subspecies can make delightful companions.

FINCH'S GIFTS: Ability to remain centered through periods of change, balance in the family and community, understanding the power of the voice.

FINCH CAN HELP: to gain strength during periods of unexpected change; for spiritual sustenance during a divorce or the death of a loved one.

DOVE

The word "dove" refers to about 300 hundred different species of bird, some of which are the common pigeon. Despite having the reputation of being a winged sort of rat, pigeons and their dove counterparts are incredibly intelligent. They can learn a lengthy set of actions, divide attention between two sets of stimuli, remember hundreds of images for periods of several years, and have been able to survive in an incredibly diverse array of climates and habitats.

In Greek mythology, doves were associated with the Golden Goddess from Crete, and were said to pull Aphrodite's chariot through the sky. Doves are referred to in Genesis, when Noah is trying to figure out whether land is near. The Dove is almost universally referred to as a good omen, a source of luck, or a symbol of peace.

DOVE'S GIFTS: Peace, love, gentleness, communication between two worlds.

DOVE CAN HELP: when frustrated; when struggling to remain patient; when a maternal, comforting demeanor is required.

ROADRUNNER

Roadrunners are desert-dwelling members of the cuckoo family. Though they can fly, they spend most of the time on the ground and can run at speeds of about 15 mph.

New Mexico Native American tribes told stories of Roadrunner ushering in the creation of the earth. The Mayans have a myth involving the quetzal and the roadrunner competing to be king. In the end, the quetzal gets the better of Roadrunner and his plumage is robbed of him. In some Pueblo and Apache Native American cultures, it is believed that tracing the roadrunner's tracks around a deceased person would confuse nearby evil spirits and bring good luck to the journey to spirit world..

Roadrunner Gifts: Trickery, speed, agility, endurance, connection with the desert.

Call on Roadrunner: when about to embark on a marathon of work or physical endurance; when in a place that is essentially a spiritual void.

CHICKEN

Originally from Southeast Asia, there are now more chickens in the world than there are any other bird.

To Indonesian Hindus, a chicken is considered a channel for evil spirits. One of the birds will be by the leg and kept present at a funeral ceremony to ensure that any evil spirits present go into the chicken and not the family members present.

In ancient Greece, the chicken was considered an exotic animal. Because of its valor, the cock is found as an attribute of Ares, Heracles, and Athena, and it was believed that even lions were afraid of chickens. Several of Aesop's Fables reference this belief. The birds were also quite valuable: the alleged last words of Socrates as he died were "Crito, I owe a cock to Asclepius; will you remember to pay the debt?".

In the Bible, Jesus warned of Peter's betrayal: 'I tell you, Peter, before the rooster crows today, you will deny three times that you know me.'", and earlier, Jesus compares himself to a mother hen when talking about Jerusalem: "O Jerusalem, Jerusalem, you who kill the prophets and stone those sent to you, how often I have longed to gather your children together, as a hen gathers her chicks under her wings, but you were not willing." (Matthew 23:37; also Luke 13:34).

In traditional Jewish practice, a chicken is swung around the head and then slaughtered on the afternoon before Yom Kippur. During this sacrificed, it is believed that the bird takes on all the person's sins. The meat is then donated to the poor. The death of the chicken reminds the penitent sinner that his or her life is in God's hands.

The chicken is one of the Zodiac symbols of the Chinese calendar. Also in Chinese religion, a cooked chicken as a religious offering is usually limited to ancestor veneration and worship of village deities. In Confucian Chinese Weddings, a chicken can be used as a substitute for one who is too ill to attend the ceremony. A red silk scarf is placed on the chicken's head and a close relative of the absent bride/groom holds the chicken so the ceremony may proceed.

CHICKEN'S GIFTS: The power of sunrise and the inner voice.

CHICKEN CAN HELP: when you're not sure if you should speak up or not; when tempted to procrastinate.

PARROTT

There are about 350 species of parrot in the world, most of which live in warm climates including India, southeast Asia, Southern regions of North America, South America and west Africa. The only parrots to live in the United states, the Carolina Parakeet and Thick-billed Parrot, are now extinct.

Like the crow and the jay, these birds are considered to be in the upper echelons of bird intelligence. Not only can they mimic human speech, some can associate words with meanings, and form simple sentences. A few African grays have even been taught to answer simple questions such as "how many red squares" or "how many blue circles" with astonishing accuracy.

PARROT'S GIFTS: Mockery, joy in play, admiration, mimicry, celebration of eternal sensual love, pride.

PARROT CAN HELP: to get in touch with the inner child; to better figure out which aspects of role models merit emulating; to temporarily revel in the fall of an adversary.

SPARROW

Sparrows are generally small, round birds with earth-toned feathers, and stubby little beaks. Originally Eurasian, they were introduced to the Americas by European settlers and now flourish.

The sparrow is mentioned in Christian mythology when Jesus reassures his followers that even a sparrow can't fall without God noticing. In a Japanese fable, an old man cares for a hurt sparrow, and is met by good luck and good fortune as a result of his kindness.

SPARROW'S GIFTS: Fertility, earthly desire, ability to use the power of song, joy in colors.

SPARROW CAN HELP: at the beginning, passionate stages of a relationship; when depressed and wishing to find joy in the ordinary.

CRANE

Cranes are long-necked, long-legged, graceful birds that look much like herons. Crane mythology be found in cultures coming from the Aegean, South Arabia, China, Japan and in the Native American cultures of North America. In northern Japan, the Ainu people perform ritual crane dances. In Korea, a crane dance has been performed in the courtyard of the Tongdosa Temple since 700 AD. In pre-Islamic South Arabia, the goddesses Allat, Uzza, and Manah were called the "three exalted cranes". To the Greeks, the crane was a bird of omen. In the tale of Ibycus and the cranes, Ibycus was robbed and left him for dead. Ibycus called to a flock of passing cranes, who followed the murderer and hovered over him until he finally confessed to the crime.

Aristotle describes the migration of cranes in The History of Animals, adding that the crane carries a touchstone inside it that can be used to test for gold when coughed up. A crane is considered a symbol of longevity and is often represented with other symbols of long life, such as pine, bamboo, and the tortoise in Japan and China. Vietnamese people consider crane and dragon to be symbols of their culture. In feudal Japan the crane was protected by the ruling classes and fed by the peasants. According to tradition, if one folds 1000 origami cranes one's wish for good health will be granted. Also, Legendary Taoist sages were transported between heavenly worlds on the backs of cranes.

CRANE'S GIFTS: Astral travel, longevity, elegance, connection with the past, grace.

CRANE CAN HELP: when lonely for loved ones far away; for dignity and strength in a difficult situation or ordeal.

BLACKBIRD

This solitary bird is native to Eurasia and feeds on earthworms, seeds, and berries. In Norse mythology, the blackbird, like the raven, was considered a bad omen. The Iriquois have a myth about a man who changes himself into a blackbird to woo Dawn with a song. Blackbirds appear often in Irish and Celtic mythology, where the Blackbird serves as messenger to the gods.

BLACKBIRD GIFTS: Connection to the water spirits, connection to wind spirits, power of song.
BLACKBIRD CAN HELP: when having a hard time finding your own path or voice.

LOON

The loon is a waterbird found in many parts of North America and Northern Europe. The Kwakiutl people associate the loon with fertility, copper, and wealth. The Shasta Wintu people have a myth to warn against incest. In the story, the Loon Woman falls in love with her brother and their family is plunged into flames.

LOON'S GIFTS: Connection to the ancient bird spirits, connection to spirit of the water and reeds, astral travel.

LOON CAN HELP: to jump start meditation and astral travel; when having a hard time focusing and achieving stillness.

ALBATROSS

Albatross are graceful seabirds that live in the Southern Ocean and the North Pacific. They are amongst the largest flying birds living today, and can cover great distances with minimal exertion when they ride wind currents with their enormous wingspans. They reside mainly on remote islands, usually in groups consisting of four or five pairs. Pairs mate for life, and a breeding season can take over a year to yield one egg. Currently, 19 of the 21 recognized species of albatross are endangered.

ALBATROSS'S GIFTS: Endurance, connection with spirits of the sea and the wind, loyalty, love, stamina, ability to make trash into treasure.

ALBATROSS CAN HELP: when it is necessary to improvise; to get strength to embark on a long project; to help find substitutes for things beyond your material or physical reach.

STARLING

Originally native to Europe and Asia, the starling was introduced to North America in the later half of the 19th century by a wealthy New Yorker named Eugene Schieffelin. Wishing to give North America the gift of all birds mentioned in Shakespeare plays, he let 100 starlings loose in Central Park in 1890. Those that populate the US are descended from that small group of birds.

STARLING'S GIFT: Adaptation, power of song, persuasiveness, intelligence, memory.

STARLING CAN HELP: to find the strength to speak up and speak loudly; if it is necessary to talk others into something.

SWALLOW

Swallows are agile little birds that eat insects plucked quickly out of the air. Their dynamic bodies and strong wings make them incredible fliers, and their feet are made for perching rather than walking. Usually, the male builds a nest out of mud and then attracts the female with a song. The pair remains monogamous for the duration of the mating season. In addition to being adept fliers, swallows have a flexible range of noises and songs used to attract mates, warn others of an approaching predator, or express happiness.

SWALLOW'S GIFTS: Protection, joy in song, connection to the spirit of the rain, connection to the spirit of the trees.

SWALLOW CAN HELP: when feeling stifled by an urban or oppressive environment; to connect with nature even from a concrete setting.

INSECTS AND ARACHNIDS:

BUTTERFLY

Butterflies are found in nearly every corner of the world, and the pattern on their wings tells a story of where they live and how. The Blackfoot Indians believed that dreams are brought to us on the wings of butterflies. Hopis perform elaborate butterfly dances and make clay butterflies that are said to embody the spirits of gods. The Papago peoples have a story in which the Creator gives Butterfly to children to make up for the fact that they will eventually get old and wrinkled. Bird complains that Butterfly is beautiful AND can sing prettily, so the Creator strikes Butterfly mute to please Bird. Native Americans living in Mexico by and large saw Butterfly as a spirit of rebirth and change.

In Japanese culture, butterflies forecast marital bliss, and there is an old Irish saying that butterflies are the embodiment of souls in Purgatory.

BUTTERFLY'S GIFTS: Reincarnation, transformation, transmutation, reincarnation, magick, beauty, love, transformation. Knowing and understanding the current position in the cycle of life. Divination concerning future events.

BUTTERFLY CAN HELP: when feeling lost; when about to go through a significant change in career, relationship, or other life circumstances.

BEE

In the ancient Near East and ancient Greece, bees were seen as a bridge between the natural world and the underworld, and were emblems of Potnia, the Minoan-Mycenaean "Mistress" who was sometimes called "the pure Mother Bee."Potnia was also a mother goddess to Artemis and Demeter.

The Jewish historian Josephus correctly noted that the name of the poet and prophet Deborah meant "bee". The Homeric Hymn to Apollo acknowledges that Apollo's gift of prophecy first came to him from three bee-maidens, and the Pythian pre-Olympic priestess of Delphi remained "the Delphic bee".

Beekeeping was a Minoan craft, and honey would be fermented and made into a sort of a wine. Long after Knossos fell, for two thousand years, the classical Greek tongue preserved "honey-intoxicated" as the phrase for "drunken."

The name "Merope" seems to mean "honey-faced" in Greek, thus "eloquent" in Classical times, and Cretan bee-masked priestesses appear on Minoan seals.

Currently, an unknown ailment is killing a large percentage of North American domesticated honey bees.

BEE'S GIFTS: Connection to goddesses, connection to female warrior energy, concentration, prosperity, delegation.

BEE CAN HELP: when facing challenges in fertility; to fortify oneself for a confrontation against an adversary; to learn what is best done by others and what is best done oneself.

PRAYING MANTIS

Martial art forms in China have taken plenty of inspiration from Praying Mantis. The movements inspired by Praying Mantis help the student connect with his or her chi or energy. The Mantis is gifted with its ability to ignore time, as he can stand perfectly still for as long as it takes to catch his prey.

Praying Mantis' consume large amounts of other kinds of insects, and are excellent hunters with an efficient attack strategy. Females do also devour the heads of their partners during mating.

PRAYING MANTIS GIFTS: Ability to manipulate time, power to move between minutes or seconds, female warrior energy, prowress in attack.

PRAYING MANTIS CAN HELP: if you find yourself needing to think quickly and act swiftly against an attack or adversary.

SPIDER

Spiders have in common that they are invertebrate animals that have two body segments, eight legs, no chewing mouth parts and no wings, living on every continent on Earth— even Antarctica. Most spin webs, and all but two have some form of venom used to immobilize or capture prey. Folklore is replete with stories about spiders: in Greek mythology, a young woman named Arachne claimed she could weave better than the gods, and was turned into a spider as punishment. Anansi, a West African trickster god, is often depicted as a spider. In Lakota mythology, Iktomi is a spider-trickster spirit and cultural folk hero.

SPIDER'S GIFTS: Wisdom, creativity, control over fate, divine inspiration, shapeshifting, connection with the goddess' power to give life.

SPIDER CAN HELP: when facing writer's block; when lacking in inspiration; when needing to get in touch with goddess energy.

ANT

Ants have colonized just about everywhere on earth, and the only places without native ant species are Antarctica, Iceland, Greenland, and Hawaii. They live in enormous colonies, and if all were added up, it is estimated that they would constitute 15% of the total terrestrial animal biomass. Ants all begin lives as eggs—the fertilized ones become female ants; the unfertilized ones become male ants. While in larval stages, they are fed different amounts according to what caste they will be: queen, soldier, worker, etc. Queens and workers are all female, and a Queen can live for thirty years whereas a male ant will only live a few weeks.

Some ants do not form colonies and hunt individually. Others are incapable of feeding themselves and will live off other species of ants that they capture and keep as workers/slaves.

Some Native American religions recognize ants as the very first animals; others may use ant bites in initiation ceremonies.

ANT'S GIFTS: Patience, stamina, strength, ability to store for the future, power of sacrificing self for the community.

ANT CAN HELP: when tempted to give up on a difficult but enriching task, hobby, or goal; to get guidance on how to deal with strife in the family or workplace.

LADYBUG

The ladybug is a member of the beetle family that primarily feed on aphids and other insects. The "lady" in the name "ladybug" is thought to refer to Virgin Mary. Indeed, in Norway, the ladybug is called Freyjuhaena after Freyja, the fertility goddess in Norse Mythology. In Denmak, the ladybug is called the Mary's Hen, in Turkey it is called Good Luck Bug, and in Irish, the ladybug is called God's Little Cow.

LADYBUG'S GIFTS: Past lives, spiritual rebirth, connection with the spirit of plants and all things that grow from the earth.

LADYBUG CAN HELP: when about to plant a garden; when planning on nurturing a project from its conception to its fruition.

ROACH

Cockroaches exist everywhere except for the polar regions, and there are currently about 3500 living species today. They are omnivores, and a single female can produce 300 to 400 offspring throughout the course of her life. Arab physicians in the 9th century advocated grinding them up to use as medication, saying that they would cure earaches, open wounds, and gynecological disorders.

ROACH'S GIFTS: Survival, speed, ability to cause fear and disgust, understanding darkness and shadows.

ROACH CAN HELP: to intimidate adversaries; when feeling consumed by a shadow that will not lift any time soon.

SCORPION

Scorpions are a variety of arachnid with 6 to 8 legs, claws, and a tail, primarily living in desert regions. All scorpions are cold-blooded, and all are capable of injecting venom into their prey, usually a type of venom that has the potential to induce paralysis.

When scorpions mate, the male takes the female by her pincers, and they do a sort of an dance. He will then lead her to a suitable location to deposit his spermatophore, and she will walk over it several times so her eggs will be fertilized by it. Occasionally the male will be eaten by the female, so after mating is over, the male usually hurries away.

There is an Afghan folktale in which an eagle carries away the shoe of the prophet Mohammed. When a scorpion falls out of the shoe, he returns it to Mohammed, thus saving him from its bite. Ancient Egyptians at one time believed that scorpions came from the corpses of crocodiles, and that women were immune to the sting of the scorpion.

SCORPION'S GIFTS: Surprise attack, reflecting dark energy back to the sender, connection with poison.

SCORPION CAN HELP: when a threat is imminent; when facing aggression from a potential adversary or assailant.

TARANTULA

The tarantula is a large, hairy arachnid that doesn't spin webs, and lives on the ground. Various species of tarantula can be found in the Southern parts of the US, South America, the Mediterranean basin, Africa, Southeast Asia, and Australia. They can eat insects, small mice, or small fish. There are poisonous species of tarantula in South America that can induce paralysis in humans, or a coma-like state.

The bite of a Taranula was once believed to cause tarantism, whose cure, according to folk medicine, involve wild dancing similar to the tarantella. There appears to have indeed existed a species of spider in the fields around Taranto responsible for fairly severe bites.

TARANTULA'S GIFTS: Transformation, creativity, intimidation with size and brute force, ability to use the environment to hide rather than go forth in aggression.

TARANTULA CAN HELP: to prepare to confront an adversary on your own turf.

MOSQUITO

The first mosquito appeared in South America during the Jurassic Period. The Mayans have a tale about two boys that use a mosquito to puncture a jug and steal water. Mosquito also has a place in Mayan mythology as a trickster and a spy. The Tuscarora Indians have a story involving a large, monstrous mosquito that was eventually vanquished and split into tiny versions of itself. The Lakota people also have a story in which Mosquito was originally large, but made tiny after he felled a sapling with his giant lancet.

MOSQUITO'S GIFTS: Connection with water, ability to heal diseases of the blood, stealth.

MOSQUITO CAN HELP: to meditate during illness; when it is necessary to keep a secret.

CRICKET

The cricket is an insect somewhat related to grasshoppers and katydids. The male of the species is capable of emitting a chirping sound that varies along with the ambient temperature. One can calculate the temperature in Fahrenheit by adding the number 39 to however many chirps can be counted in 15 seconds.

The singing of crickets in the folklore of Brazil is taken to be a sign of impending rain, or of good financial fortune.

In Caraguatatuba, Brazil, a black cricket in a room is said to indicate illness; a gray one money; and a green one hope.

In Alagoas state, northeast Brazil, a cricket announces death, and in the village of Capueiruçu, Bahia State, a constantly chirping cricket foretells pregnancy. The mole cricket is also said to predict rain when it digs into the ground.

In Barbados, a loud cricket means predicts that a financial windfall will soon follow.

In Zambia, the cricket brings good luck to anyone who sees it.

CRICKET'S GIFTS: Good luck, power of song, connection with the weather, strength to work one's way out of darkness.

CRICKET CAN HELP: to find joy in your own voice; when preparing for a heat wave or a harsh winter.

FIREFLY

This type of beetle is so named because of its unique ability to produce cold, UV free rays of light to attract mates or prey.

Fireflies were a part of ancient Mayan mythology, and may have had at least one representative in the pantheon of Mayan gods. The ancient Chinese sometimes captured fireflies in transparent or semi-transparent containers and used them as lanterns. Firefly is also a character in a Western African fable that warns against the consequences of selfishness.

FIREFLY'S GIFTS: Ability to guide others, ability to find light in darkness, ability to create and spread good energy.

FIREFLY CAN HELP: when struggling to be an effective leader; when facing discontent amongst the ranks of those being led.

GRASSHOPPER

Grasshoppers are very similar to crickets, however, are unable to chirp. In Greek mythology, Selene, the moon goddess, turned a mortal into a grasshopper when he began to age.

According to the Bible, a swarm of locusts—a type of grasshopper—descended from the sky in the story of the plagues of Egypt. The Book or Revelation states that locusts with scorpion tails and human faces are to torment unbelievers for five months when the fifth trumpet sounds. Another plague, according to Joel, will consist of "swarming locusts, cutting locusts, hopping locusts and destroying locusts." This fits with the many stages of locust developtment: the "hopper" probably denotes the nymph stage.

In Plato's Phaedrus, Socrates says that locusts were once human. When the Muses first brought song into the world, the beauty so captivated some people that they forgot to eat and drink until they died. The Muses turned those unfortunate souls into locusts— singing their entire lives.

GRASSHOPPER GIFTS: Ability to take leap of faith, astral travel, ability to easily traverse large obstacles or voids in one's path.

GRASSHOPPER CAN HELP: when taking a big chance; when facing a significant obstacle to achieving a goal or dream

DRAGONFLY

The prey of a dragonfly can not escape by diving away because dragonflies typically attack from below.

The dragonfly live starts in the water and ends on land.

In Europe, dragonflies are sometime seen as evil, having to hold the souls of people for the devil.

For some Native American tribes dragonflies represent swiftness and activity, and for the Navajo they symbolize pure water.
It is said in some Native American beliefs that dragonflies are a symbol of renewal after a time of great hardship.

In Japan dragonflies are symbols of courage, strength, and happiness,

Vietnamese people forecast rain by seeing dragonflies.

Dragonfly people can be emotional and passionate as youngsters, then transforming into adults with great control and mental clarity.

Dragonfly Gifts: Light, Change, Wisdom, Enlightenment, courage, strength, happiness, swiftness and activity

Call on Dragonfly: When you need changing or need to see a pathway to transformation,

REPTILES AND AMPHIBIANS:

TOAD

Toads share a large amount of characteristics with frogs. True toads, however, have skin that looks somewhat warty, and have glands in the backs of their heads that can secrete poison. One type of toxin secreted by toads can be used by humans as a psychedelic drug.

The Cochiti people have a myth in which a toad and a bird play hide and seek. The Lakota tell a tale about a toad that cared for a young boy that had been separated from his tribe. The Miwok tell a story about Toad-woman taken against her will as Bird's wife, and the Micmac have a fable telling about Toad losing his nose because of his pride.

TOAD'S GIFTS: Connection to altered states of consciousness, connection with earth and water spirits, changing luck.

TOAD CAN HELP WHEN: when it looks like a disappointment is on the horizon; to aid in more productive meditation.

FROG

The frog is remarkably adaptable, living everywhere from the tropics to the sub-arctic. Sadly, one third of all frog species are believed to be threatened with extinction. The Tlingit people have a legend about a woman that married a frog and taught her own people to treat frogs with respect. The Cree have a legend about a frog that burrowed beneath the earth to escape a giant cannibal. The Alsea people have a rather sexually charged myth in which coyote steals the vulvas of two frog women by tricking them into sticking their heads into a bag filled with bees.

FROG'S GIFTS: Transformation, cleansing, rebirth, the power of song.

FROG CAN HELP: when about to experience a major life change.

SNAKE

Mythology concerning snakes and serpents can be found a wide range of religions and regions of the world. The Hopi people of North America perform an annual snake dance to celebrate the union of Snake and Snake Girl. At the end of the dance, snakes were released into the fields to bring good luck to the harvest and encourage fertility.

Many peoples in Africa and Australia had myths about a Rainbow Snake which either gave birth to all animals, and created rivers, creeks and oceans. In ancient Indian myth, the snake Ahi swallowed the primordial ocean and did not release all created beings until his stomach was split with a thunderbolt. In another Hindu myth, the creator Brahma slept on the coils of the world-serpent Shesha. Indian mythology also tells of nagas and naginis--human-headed snakes whose kings and queens lived in a jewel-encrusted underground.

Greek myths tell a snake caring for the egg from which all created things were born. In Egyptian myth, the state of existence before creation was symbolised as Amduat, a many-coiled serpent. The Gorgons of Greek myth were snake-women who could turn adversaries into stone. it.

In an Egyptian myth, Aapep attacked the sun every morning and wouldn't succeed until nightfall. Egyptian myth has had several snake-gods, from the 'coiled one' Mehen to the two-headed Nehebkau who guarded the underworld.

In Nordic myth, evil was symbolized by a serpent who coiled around one of the three roots of the Tree of Life, and tried to choke the life from

The Aztec underworld was protected by python-trees, and the Brule Sioux people told of three brothers transformed into rattlesnakes which helped and guided humans.

The Pomo people told of a woman who married a rattlesnake-prince and gave birth to four snake-children, and the Hopi people told of a young man who ventured into the underworld and married a snake-princess.

The Navajo tell of Glispa, a girl returned with special powers spending two years with the Snake People. The Aztec spirit of intelligence, Quetzalcoatl was a plumed snake, and Mayans told of a goddess whose snake companions would whisper the secrets of the universe. Rivers and lakes also often had snake-gods or snake-guardians including Untekhi, the protector of the Missouri River.

Carved stones depicting a seven-headed Cobra are commonly found near the sluices of the ancient irrigation tanks in Sri Lanka, and it is theorized that they served as guardians of water.

SNAKE'S GIFTS: Elusiveness, manipulation, transmutation, mystery, goddess energy, protection from religious persecution, immortality, connection to soul world.

SNAKE CAN HELP: when it is necessary to lie in wait for events to unfold; to connect psychically with a loved one who has passed; to strengthen faith.

TORTOISE

This long-lived, slow-moving reptile is one of the four symbols of Chinese constellations. The Tortoise is known as the Black Warrior from the North and represents the winter. The Black Tortoise corresponds with seven positions of the moon. In ancient China, the tortoise and the snake were thought of as the symbols of longevity. During the Han Dynasty, people often wore tortoise pendants made of jade. In Japan, too, important titles and badges of honor often referred to the tortoise or images of tortoises.

A legend eventually arose that said that female tortoises were only able to copulate with male snakes. From then on, men whose wives were having extramarital affairs were often referred to as "tortoises," and so people stopped using the tortoise as a symbol of good luck.
Tortoises have also been identified as one of four benevolent animals that decorated the gardens of the Yellow Emperor.

TORTOISE'S GIFTS: Connection with the earth, connection with centeredness, power to heal female diseases, tenacity, non-violent defense, patience, wisdom.

TORTOISE CAN HELP: when confused about the intentions of others, when patience is required, when preparing for a confrontation with a boss or authority figure.

SALAMANDER

Salamanders are amphibians primarily found in moist habitats. Due to their adaptive nature, it appears frequently in mythology. In Medieval Europe renderings of salamanders include depictions as a winged dog and as bursting into flames.

Pliny the Elder wrote that the a salamander is "an animal like a lizard in shape and with a body starred all over; it never comes out except during heavy showers and disappears the moment the weather becomes clear". Pliny also claims that salamanders can put out a fire with the frigidity of their bodies, and describes medicinal and poisonous properties, claiming that a single salamander running around a tree it could poison the fruit.
As species of salamander hibernate in rotting and dead wood, plenty of opportunities sprang for creative embellishment of their capabilities: when was brought indoors and put on the fire, the creatures mysteriously appeared from the flames. According to some writers, the

milky substance that a salamander exudes when frightened and which makes its skin very moist gave rise to the idea that the salamander could withstand any heat and even put out fires.

The salamander is mentioned in the Talmud as being a product of fire, and anyone who is smeared with its blood will be immune to harm from fire. Additionally, the Talmud claims that a salamander is produced by burning a fire in the same place for seven years. According to hadith, Muhammad said that salamanders are "mischief-doers" and "should be killed".

SALAMANDER'S GIFTS: Connection to both Earth and water gods, comfort in the face of change, adaptability, beauty.

SALAMANDER CAN HELP: when it is necessary to adapt to a new or unfamiliar situation.

FISH AND OTHER CREATURES OF THE SEA:

FISH

Through the ages, many cultures have featured fish in their legends and myths, from the "great fish" that swallowed Jonah the Prophet through to the half-human, half-fish mermaid around which books and movies have been centered.

Among the fish gods and goddesses said are Ika-Roa of the Polynesians, Dagon of the ancient Semitic peoples, and Matsya of the Dravidas of India. Ichthys were used by early Christians to identify themselves, and the fish remains a symbol of fertility among Bengalis

In Japan, where koi ponds are abundant, the koi is seen as a symbol of perseverance, luck, and success. According to Chinese mythology a carp which succeeds in swimming upstream through rapids of the Yangtze River will be transformed into a dragon.

Carp Kites flown in Japan on 'Boys Day' are still a very important part of traditional celebrations. A black carp represents the male head of the family, the eldest son gets a red carp, and all successive sons receive progressively smaller carp. In Japanese mythology, a shachihokoan was a powerful, mythological animal with the head of a tiger and the body of a carp. It was believed that this animal could bring rain, and images of the animal could be found in temples and homes to protect the occupants from fire.

Under the tropical zodiac, Pisces is occupied by the Sun from February 20 to March 20, and under the sidereal zodiac, it is currently from March 15 to April 13. The opposite sign to Pisces is Virgo.

FISH GIFTS: Fertility, grace, connection to the water god, ability to heal others, ability to find energy from stillness, love, harmony.
CALL ON FISH: when preparing to start a family, before journeying over water; to cope with the illness of a loved one; to aid in fruitful meditative practices.

SALMON

Salmon are closely related to trout, and though they are born in freshwater, migrate to the ocean, and then return to fresh water to reproduce. As of late, wild salmon populations have been in decline due to overfishing.

The Salmon of Wisdom appears in Irish mythology as an ordinary salmon that ate the nine hazel nuts that fell into the Fountain of Wisdom from nine hazel trees that surrounded the fountain. In doing so, the salmon gained all the knowledge in the world. Moreover, the first person to eat of its flesh would, in turn, gain this knowledge.

In Finnish mythology, the maiden Aino drowned herself rather than marry, and returned from the dead as a salmon.

SALMON'S GIFTS: Connection with home and hearth, strength to swim upstream, rebirth of spirit.

SALMON CAN HELP: to get strength for a difficult spiritual or physical ordeal; when struggling to remain centered in a sea of temptations.

OCTOPUS

Octopi have eight arms and almost entirely soft bodies with no internal skeleton. They have no sharp claws, no jaw full of teeth, no ability to secrete poison or a cloud of ink. A beak is the only hard part of their body. This enables octopi to fit through very narrow crevices in order to escape potential predators. Some species live for as little as six months. Males can only live for a few months after mating, and females starve to death shortly after their eggs hatch because they don't eat when taking care of the unhatched eggs.

Octopi have three hearts and blue-colored blood. Two pump blood through each of the two gills, while the third heart pumps blood through the body.

OCTOPUS GIFTS: Intelligence, ability to use smoke and mirrors to evade capture.

OCTOPUS CAN HELP: when about to get into a potentially combative or tense situation with an adversary; to figure out ways to use brains rather than brawn to get out of a difficult situation.

SHARK

The fossil record shows that the first shark came in to
existence around 100 million years ago. In December 2001,
a pup was born from a female hammerhead shark who had
not been in contact with a male shark for over three years.
It was later confirmed that sharks can reproduce without
mating. Sharks have an extremely acute sense of smell, and
some can even detect as little as one part blood per million
parts of seawater from a quarter of a mile away. It has
recently been shown that sharks are extremely bright and
possess surprisingly good problem solving skills. Shark's
intelligence, keen sense of smell, and powerful jaws make
him a very efficient predator.

Sharks have figured very prominently in Hawaiian
mythology and several shark gods and goddesses appear in
the Hawaiian pantheon. Kamohoali'i is the best known
and revered of the shark gods, and was able to take on all
human and fish forms. The goddess Ka'ahupahau was born
a human and later transformed into a shark. Kane'apua
was a trickster god and the brother of Pele and
Kamohoali'i. Dakuwanga was a shark god who was the
eater of lost souls.

SHARK'S GIFTS: Connection with the sea gods, ability to move constantly, pride in the family, remorselessness, ability to attack, connection to past knowledge, ability to inspire fear.

SHARK CAN HELP: when it may be necessary to defend self and family fearlessly; when a difficult but necessary task—such as putting a pet to sleep, or ceasing to enable an addicted family member—is impending.

CPSIA information can be obtained at www.ICGtesting.com
Printed in the USA
BVOW070634191011

274026BV00001B/425/P